Ten Unique Side Hustle Ideas for the New Year

Dana Sage

Copyright © 2013 Dana Sage

All rights reserved. No part of this publication may be reproduced, stored in or introduced into a retrieval system, or transmitted, in any form, or by any means (electronic, mechanical, photocopying, recording, or otherwise) without the prior written permission of both the copyright owner and the publisher of this book. Please purchase only authorized electronic editions and do not participate in or encourage electronic piracy of copyrighted materials. Your support of the author's rights is appreciated. To contact the author email: bookinquiry@hotmail.com and place book title in subject line.

ISBN: 1494990997
ISBN-13: 978-1494990992

LETTER TO READERS

Dear Readers,

I would like to thank you for taking this opportunity in reading this book and for purchasing this book. It meant a lot for me to convey this message of the importance of having a side hustle for the new year.

In today's economy, the need for having a side hustle has grown significantly particularly within the past 10 years. Rather than just provide a list of 100 or more business opportunities, I took this opportunity to narrow it down to 10 simple and proven ideas that anyone can try without the need for having any large amount of money to get started.

In addition to all the great ideas that are provided, I've also included a free bonus list of broker priced opinion companies also known as asset management companies for those of you who are particularly interested in the real estate BPO idea.

All of the ideas provided in this book I have tried myself and have learned all of the in's and out's that would make each and every one of them a major success. Keep in mind that while these ideas can become full-time ventures they are intended to supplement current income and serve mainly as side hustles.

Thank you again for choosing this book and happy reading!

Your Author,

Dana Sage

INTRODUCTION

Napoleon Hill in the book, *Think and Grow Rich* reiterated that "Fear is the greatest single obstacle to success". He and many others who've said it before him was right. Too often people let fear hold them back from the things that they hope to attain in life. Many of them hope to achieve more yet some of them often find themselves content with mediocre. I like to call it having a "little-bit" mentality. If this sounds like you then great you've picked up the right book and there's a reason why you're reading this introduction and I hope it motivates you to change the direction of your thinking. If you have always been a mass thinker and have always been seeking ways to earn more for your future that is awesome because that means that you are without a doubt motivated and will get started head on with the opportunities and ideas discussed in this book and fear will not be an issue.

This is the year to put fear behind you and to take control of where your lives are financially. In this book I'm not going to give you some cliché advice on working smart and not working hard. You can expect honesty throughout and legitimate side hustle opportunities that not only promote increase in wealth but also savings opportunities as well. The advice however that I am going to give you is to simply consider your financial future and ask yourself if you are making decisions that are preparing you for that financial security that you want and need.

I expect people who read this book to either be employed and looking for a side hustle or are unemployed and considering

TEN UNIQUE SIDE HUSTLE IDEAS FOR THE NEW YEAR

entrepreneurial opportunities because they are tired of giving employers and others the say-so on how they earn their living. For older generations that may be reading this book, you might recall a time in American society when having a job was golden. Having a job meant security and today after the crushing and debilitating blow to the U.S. economy within the past thirteen years it's safe to say that a J-O-B now means being "Just Over Broke". Forget trying to make it to the middle class with having one job.

In recent years we've seen people who should be enjoying retirement go back to work in jobs they least expected themselves working in to supplement their eleven hundred dollar a month social security income. Is this because they failed to succeed? Absolutely not! It's because unfortunately when things were looking up with the economy, they failed to plan. This is why I stress the importance of having a side hustle and embracing the idea of having multiple income streams particularly those that are passive income streams that can help you to save for your future.

There are some money making opportunities that I'd like to mention briefly that are not covered in this book that I feel is worth mentioning before I even get started. Knowing what it is to be young, broke and unemployed from experience and knowing what having bad credit feels like, I'd like to stress to you the importance of the following money making or rather financial planning ventures I'm about to discuss with you right now.

Firstly, if you have bad credit, this year is the year to fix it. Designate any tax refunds and job bonuses that you may have towards paying off your debt or at least try to settle them with the creditors. Remember that credit gets better when you can establish new credit so start with a secured credit card and work your credit up from there. In the long run your credit score will improve but you'll have to take care of those in collections first. Credit is still important for future financial success.

Secondly, and this goes out to young people in their 20's, 30's, 40's and as young as you feel. Stocks are not just for rich people. When I first started off investing in stocks, I invested through Share Builder, paid a small fee of six ninety-five for each trade and within three months had earned well over five hundred dollars in stock dividends after only an initial investment of one hundred dollars. While you may consider this to be "small time", how many can say that they earned over four hundred dollars over a three month period without having to do anything for it? For the young, broke and unemployed, this is a good start so begin looking into online trading platforms and start investing into stocks that interest you. If you like the iPhone don't spend six hundred on the phone, spend the six hundred on the apple stock (APPL) and watch your earnings grow when others flock to purchase the new and latest iPhone.

Thirdly, for those of you who are in your jobs and are lucky enough to still get a company match in your 401k despite the turn of the economy, please tell me that you are taking advantage of it. This is free money that you cannot afford to turn down even if you're far away from retirement. Also if you leave your job do not cash it in for a new purchase. Transfer it to another 401k if you change jobs or open an IRA with it so it can continue to grow as a future investment.

Lastly, consider looking into life insurance. You cannot imagine a difference a year makes when shopping for life insurance. I recently was asked to help someone in their late sixties obtain quotes for life insurance and the most he could get based on his age and what he could afford was thirty thousand dollars with a monthly payment of one hundred and forty-five dollars. The average thirty year old could pay thirty to fifty dollars a month for the rest of their life for a policy that would produce one hundred and fifty thousand dollars upon their death. Now with this in mind, wouldn't you rather like to start a life insurance policy before it starts costing an arm and a leg especially if you have a family?

You see, earning extra money does not only come from businesses and side hustle opportunities, it also comes from the financial decisions we make at present that can affect our financial future. I hope that these ten ideas discussed in this book are utilized and turned into profitable opportunities for each and every one of you. Some may be a good fit and others may not and you may just like one of these ideas in particular. However I can assure you that each one has the potential as a side hustle to become your main hustle if you decide to put your own spin on these ideas and develop them into massive money making ventures. So good luck and if you're ready let's get started on a side hustle today.

ROTATING SAVINGS CLUB "SUSU"

So that there's no excuse to getting started with your side hustle, I deliberately included this idea as a side hustle, extra money making idea first to give anyone the opportunity to get cash in hand that can be used toward building any money making venture. As with most money making ideas some capital is often needed. While those mentioned in this book require very little if any startup capital, it's a great idea to have aside at least some savings when starting any venture and a rotating savings club (Susu) is a great and unique way to get started.

So, have you heard of a susu savings club? If not it's because it's a known practice often used by African and Caribbean communities here in the U.S and abroad. When I was little girl growing up on the island of Trinidad, I remember my mother getting really excited when it was her turn for a payout in her susu group. As a matter of fact, when we migrated to the United States, my mother was able to continue this practice with a group of fellow Caribbean people in Brooklyn, New York.

Many people use a susu savings club to pay for vacations, weddings, to purchase a car, start a business, pay for other expenses and a whole lot more. A susu savings club is a great way to get the cash that you need to get your side hustle on the go.

So what is this susu I keep talking about? A susu is a savings club consisting of a small group of people who pool together a specific amount of money for a set period of time; distributing the cash pot as a payout to their members each at a set schedule. Forbes.com listed a few online susu's started by businesses which you can get involved in if you don't want to start your own club. Emoneypool.com and yattos.com are a couple notable ones you can review online for yourself.

Members often pick when they'll receive they're cash payout. They provide an annual payout in one month for each participant. I should also note that susu groups are not illegal and you will not have to report it to the IRS since it is a savings of your already earned income that you will report at tax time so there is no need to report it as additional earnings.

Let me show you how this works. Let's say a dozen people in a new susu group contribute $100 a month for a whole year. In the first month of the pot, member A gets well... $1200. Member B gets $1200 the following month and so on and so on until each person has contributed $1200 and received $1200. Every month $1200 is collected and one person in the susu group takes home all the cash. The rotation will end when everyone has had a payout of the cash pot.

Imagine if this was $400 per month per member, the cash payout would be $4800 each month to each member when their time is up to receive the cash payout. The more members the more money, the least amount of members, the quicker the payout and the rotation. Now no loss no gain I know but the point is when you first paid your $100 did you have $1200 cash in hand to begin with at that specific time? Or if you were sixth in line to receive the cash pot and already paid in $600 wouldn't $600 more cash be helpful to you? This is why susus are so popular in those aforementioned communities. It's like borrowing money within your group, receiving a cash payout sooner rather than later, minus the interest and taxes all while paying it back within the allotted time.

Now I know you must be wondering, what if I'm the banker and I went last after paying out $1200 for the whole year? How does that benefit me since I don't get an early payout? If you are the pot holder (also known as the banker) and you went last this year make sure your group agrees for you to be the first in line to receive the pot the following year. So how does $2400 in hand feel

TEN UNIQUE SIDE HUSTLE IDEAS FOR THE NEW YEAR

for the start of the new year? Or with the $4800 example, how does $9600 feel for the new year? Each year after that as the pot holder you can alternate between first and last payouts to be fair with everyone else in your group. Just make sure as the pot holder you're honest with cash payouts and your members are trustworthy and reliable to make their contribution timely. With your cash payout you can even start another money making venture that we'll talk about next and turn that $1200 into 12,000 or more.

LEASE OPTIONS

Have you ever wanted to get into real estate investing without having to worry about the sales and licensing aspect of the field? Well this is a unique opportunity in the real estate industry that can make you money in real estate without the risk and obligations of home ownership and the best part is that it is perfectly legal. As a matter of fact I should mention that everything that is in this book is perfectly legal, personally tried and proven and comes with my stamp of approval in terms of profit and earnings potential.

These are not get rich quick schemes or pyramid schemes that can get you in trouble but actual money making ventures that many do not talk about because they would rather not share how it is they make their money in hopes of keeping ideas like these on the low-low. Those that do share this technique make money selling the information through CDs and DVDs on infomercials and conventions without actually giving people the information they need to get started to succeed. So here it is without the subscriptions and convention travel expenses – make money in real estate without having to sell or earn a real estate license.

A lease option in real estate is another way of saying "lease with option to purchase" or what is more commonly referred to as a "Rent to Own" home. What a lease option provides is an agreement to lease a property with an option to buy it at a fixed price at a predetermined time when the lease option is signed. That is you agree to a sales price and time in lease upfront regardless of whether or not the value of the home increases. The owner cannot change the agreed upon price if there's a value increase in the home. Typically there is a small up front down payment that looks more like a small deposit that can range from $1 to the price of the agreed monthly lease amount (or rent) or can be as large as 3% of the fixed price to 5% down depending on the seller's agreed upon terms. Either way it's usually negotiable and can vary.

The lease can last from one year to two years and the good news is, at the end of the term, the lessee, the person renting to own the home, does not have to buy the home at the end of the lease but will however forfeit any deposit and earned equity in the home if they don't eventually buy it. The longer the term the better the deal because it gives you an opportunity to gain financing and purchase the home at the end of the lease option contract unless of course you had no issue with financing to begin with. In the end you would have owned your own home, earned equity in the home if its value increased and would have paid only a small down payment and monthly rent with a chance to actually live in the home and test drive the community and neighbors before purchasing it.

Now what if you want to earn money with lease options as an investor and not actually live in the home? Now this is where lease options can earn you income and the best part is, it is commonly practiced among real estate investors. If you want to earn money as a lease option investor, the first thing I recommend you do is to find you a real estate agent who works lease options as their niche or is at least interested in lease option sales. When I started my business "Low Country Lease Options LLC" in South Carolina, I made a seasoned real estate agent my business partner and brought her all the prospective buyers which we qualified with a one year term requirement. Within three months we had already signed up 30 people by tax season and I wasn't even a real estate agent at the time. Because I was not a real estate agent I was able to charge a finder's fee to the homeowners of $1000 of their asking deposit payable upon signing the lease option. This fee was for matching the sellers to buyers for rent to own homes, negotiating terms and assisting renters with financing opportunities with access to my agent's resources. The agent gained a commission at the end of the term with the sale of the home that she helped them buy, and it was a win-win for everyone involved. Finding rent to own homes and working with a realtor as a business partner is one way to make money with lease options.

Another way to make money with lease options is to actually lease the home yourself and sublet it to a third party. Just note that you are still responsible for the monthly lease if you sublet. Sort of like the way a landlord who rents is still responsible for paying that mortgage so sublet responsibly and do your due diligence with background checks on your sublets. For example, say you were offered a lease option for a set home sales price of $100,000 for a two year term at $1500 down and $775 per month. You manage to negotiate a better deal, you decide to tell the homeowner "hey, what if I paid $3500 down and $575 per month with the right to a sublease".

Now if you are going to eventually own this home, you should have that right. Right? Now with the right to a sublease, you can sublet the home to a renter with a 12 month lease whichever is agreed upon by you and the renter in writing but instead of renting it out for $575/month you'll rent it at the market rent of $775/month with a $775 deposit because the market value in that area is averaging out around the $700's. Not only are you making an extra $200/month but you've managed to secure a renter in the home that is paying the monthly lease option. You've also earned back $775 of your $3500 deposit and by the end of twelve months, would have made $2400 on your sublease.

Can you imagine if you had been managing 10 of these subleases and earning the same amount every month. That would mean $24,000/year in sublease earnings which you can actually use toward the purchase of your own home. And the best part is that subleasing is typically allowed in most states if not all of them. My recommendation would be to inquire with your state's laws on subletting property just to make sure you are compliant. The only work you have to put into it is finding and negotiating the right deal and have a small to medium sized down payment for leverage on the monthly rent. The higher the down payment you make the more leverage and negotiating room you have in this type of side hustle.

With lease options, it's all about negotiating the agreement because in real estate everything is negotiable and don't you forget it. Lease options can be found anywhere and in any community and sometimes can be done with family members who are unable to sell their home or with friends as an investment opportunity or group investment effort. No matter how they are obtained, it's a great and unique way to get started in real estate without the practice of selling real estate.

PUBLISHING EBOOKS FOR KINDLE, NOOK AND IPAD

Now this one is for the individual with a creative side who has a unique ability to convey their creative in literary form. If anyone has ever told you that you should write a book one day because you have a message or story to tell then you should know that it is easier to publish a book today than ever before.

Do you remember when getting a book deal meant writing a manuscript, getting a literary agent and hoping for your phone to ring with good news of getting published but only after receiving a hundred rejection letters? Well that still exists however with Amazon, Barnes and Noble and other platforms allowing regular people like you and me to self-publish, e-book publishing has become increasingly more popular.

Companies like Lulu, Amazon's Create Space, Nook and Blurb to name a few, understand that with the changing economy and myriad of talent that exists can be discovered through the platforms that they provide and here's the kicker...most of these publishing platforms allow you to self-publish for very little or no cost!

The reason why e-book self-publishing is so popular is because it provides an outlet as mentioned before for creativity and it also gives you an opportunity to earn passive income which is income you can earn even while you sleep. As with any opportunity the more you put into it, the more you get out of it so it would benefit the e-book writer to at least market their book and get it noticed even on social media to increase sales. However for the individual who just likes to write, the more e-books you have out there the more money you stand to make regardless of your marketing efforts. So you see the potential for this opportunity to be a unique passive income opportunity.

If you'd like to publish your book I recommend starting with Amazon's Create Space website located at createspace.com. There you can give your book a title, receive a free ISBN and design your book cover and the best part is that it costs absolutely nothing to self-publish your book for Amazon print and Amazon Kindle. This platform even allows you to proofread online after submission compared to having to order and pay for a proof by mail. All you have to do is price your book fairly and expect when a sale is made for the publisher to take a small percentage of that sale. These e-book sales can add up and can add a significant value to your side hustle portfolio of income producing opportunities.

When you complete a manuscript for submission, you will want to make sure that it is well written, proofread and edited before you release the book and you'll also want to go to copyright.gov to apply for a copyright in order to protect your written work. A copyright which you may already know, prevents others from stealing and claiming your written work.

If you'd like to self-publish for Barnes and Noble's Nook, then visit nookpress.com and use that site to get started. Maybe you're more of an iPad type user and you'll like to publish e-books for iPads, then blurb.com offers a fantastic opportunity to create books in print and e-books for iPads. Blurb at this time however, does not allow e-books for Kindle and Nook. Each one of these platforms has its pros and cons and after trying them out you'll eventually decide on using all or considering a preferred method that you believe works best.

My advice is the more books you produce, the more money you can make. The more you market your book on social media the more money you can make! Either way there is money to be made in writing e-books! May I suggest that if you do write e-books, try to offer books in the same genre. It wouldn't make sense that you write inspirational books only to suddenly switch gears and start offering books on true crime. And if you do want to write in different genre's consider using a separate pen name to separate your raunchy writing from your professional writing in your own name. Many writers do it all the time. Also if you need photos for your book cover consider purchasing stock photography online. Websites like shutterstock.com and istockphoto.com are great places to get started with photos and other illustrations.

Just know that the money you make is taxable if you make more than $600 a year in e-book sales and yes, Uncle Sam will know you got paid for your e-book sales because Amazon and NookPress will send you a 1099-MISC for your book royalties. So what do you do from here? Start writing then go get paid!

PRIVATE LABEL

Ever wanted to start a skin care or hair care product business? With the latest trend of natural hair and an increase in hair care and skin care products for women, why wouldn't you want a piece of this action? To get an idea of this business, think of natural hair care product guru, Carol's Daughter or popular makeup artist Danessa Myrick's makeup line IMYB. They know all about private labels and getting their brand out there to the consumer. If you look at youtube videos all you see are videos on natural hair, makeup and even some on body scrubs, skin peels and hair extensions. So how can you get started with your very own product line?

You can start by using a Private Label company? The best part is, you can start this business on a shoe-string budget! You can use private labeling for skin care, hair care and even makeup products and you don't have to worry about packaging, formulas, FDA regulations and all those details because the private label company does all of that for you.

So what is the Private Label side hustle opportunity? Private labeling is a type of product purchase system whereby you can have your own brand name on a product manufactured by a company that will supervise the process, manufacture the product and even package the product. Many of these companies help you with package design and mass distribution, others will consider minimum orders and drop shipping. The key is to do a little research and find one that best suits your money and time management needs.

With product labeling you get to: Have your own brand name on your product. You won't have to worry about whipping up products in your kitchen and you can start marketing them for shelving and sales. If you're a makeup artist or hair dresser, you can upsell your brand name products in your company name to your clients inside your own personal establishment and can use social media such as youtube to demonstrate the use, quality and value of your products on your channel.

Other than youtube, how can I reach people to buy my product you ask? Well let's say for example you started a facebook page called "Natural Women Natural Hair" and after a while you now have 10,000 likes. That is 10,000 people that get your updates on your facebook page or as some like to call it…10,000 fans! Because you specifically blog about natural hair care, that's become your niche. So you decide to launch "Natural Women Hair Care Serum" with your very own label and your very own logo. That one product can now be marketed to those 10,000 fans and you can even do giveaways and have people provide reviews on your product. In the end, it's your name, your business, your product, your success!

My advice…if you're just starting off in this business, start small with one or two products on your product line that you yourself have used and like, then work your way up to guru status whereby you can expand the line. Many celebrities get into this as well with perfumes and lotions. Take Tia and Tamera and their try at launching a lotion product line together. They're not making the products themselves, they went to a product label to slap their name on the manufacturer's product and because of their name, they're likely to become very successful from it. So why not you?

Popular niches to consider in this business are hair care products and makeup products for women. In this business, a niche will make you rich! For an example of a private label opportunity see the following link: http://youtu.be/AoWLAsqAJU8 for pinnaclecosmetics.com. Cosmetic Laboratories of America is another leader in the industry and there's many more online. Just type in "private label" as a keyword online and research them to get started.

FREELANCE MAKEUP ARTIST

It used to be that becoming a makeup artist meant going to a reputable school in New York, California or Florida and launching out during Fashion Week in Milan if you were lucky enough to intern or be a known artist. Okay I may have exaggerated a bit here but you get my point. Makeup artistry involved some process of certification and a sixty hour licensing course in aesthetics and hundreds if not thousands for a program that likely led to you doing it as a side gig anyways.

Today, makeup artistry is all over the internet with opportunities to learn and get certified from home and some are even self-taught thanks to…yet again…youtube and other places I'll discuss further in this chapter!

Take for example Tatiana Ward known to her youtube fans as *BeatFaceHoney*. Let me just say that I absolutely adore and am a big fan of her work. She's real, down to earth and is a self-taught makeup artist. Her youtube channel showcasing her makeup art gave her an opportunity to eventually get discovered by R&B super star Brandy which led to her working with other celebrities in the music industry and a career many seasoned and well trained makeup artists can only dream of. Her side hustle we can safely say has blown up to magnificent heights all because of her passion and her starting it as a side hustle.

Do you like makeup? Have you ever wanted to learn how to do your own makeup or do other people's makeup for fun? I don't about you guys but I'm a huge fan of makeup and I love watching makeup tutorials on youtube. As a matter of fact, makeup tutorials are exactly how I got started in makeup artistry. There are even courses on Udemy.com on makeup techniques.

Most makeup artists these days are self-taught but many do have some formal training in their artistry and there are a number of ways in which you can learn and perfect the skills of makeup artists. First you'd want to check your state guidelines for working as a makeup artist in your area. While most states do not require you to have a license some do if you are going to work in a salon or other professional establishment. However this section is about freelancing and not about going to work for someone else so most states in that regard do not require you to have a license if you're simply moonlighting in your spare time as a makeup artist. Hands down, makeup artistry is one of the best side hustles ever, especially if you love makeup!

Let's say that you want formal training but you don't have time to go to a school that specializes in makeup artistry. QC Makeup Academy has an online program that I recommend to get you started. And they even provide as part of the program your first makeup kit. In this program you'll not only learn color theory and techniques, you'll gain hands on experience because the course requires you to work on models of your choosing. This means having fun with family members and getting a jump start on the materials needed to start your business.

Since we're on the topic of family members, a face is a face. So don't be afraid to ask family to help you with building your portfolio. You may have a relative that has a function to attend and you can be the one to do their makeup. You can also have family refer your services initially for free or at a low competitive cost since you're now starting out. Make sure you have a digital camera handy and proper lighting to take pictures of your models for your portfolio and consider putting a professional album together using the pictures in an e-book that you can do for yourself through blurb.com picture books or mixbook.com. As you can see e-books can also be used for marketing other side hustles as well.

Another way to get started is to try to partner with a freelance photographer who is new in the business as well. New photographers are typically very happy for an opportunity to work with makeup artists because it allows them to build their own portfolio of models you bring to them as well as upsell makeup services with models they bring to you. You can create many of these partnerships by going to modelmahem.com or gigsalad.com. Those are two of my favorites. Also if you only want to do wedding makeup, advertise your services at bridal shops and on online forums such as weddings.com. Make sure if you're new and trying to build on your experience that you price your services accordingly and work your way up competitively as you become more of an expert.

Makeup artistry has been around for quite some time but with so many people learning how to do it without formal training, it's a great way to make extra money on the side by doing it for friends, family members and eventually for referrals and clients.

PRIVATE TAXI CAB LESSOR

When I was living in Charleston, South Carolina I realized something very different from that of living in Queens, New York. Transportation was not as readily available in the south as it was up north. If you've lived or now live in the southern or mid-western states you know exactly what I mean. From the looks of things, one might assume that everyone drives in these areas where transportation is grim but the truth is some people do have to rely on public transportation which poses another issue...the one time an hour bus! You miss the bus...tough luck! So what you'll find in most states are private transport companies. One day while riding in one of these private taxi cabs the driver started a conversation about how good business was and of course my business ears went up and I listened. He said that even though he was driving that taxi cab, he had another cab that he owned that was driven by someone else and while he slept at night two other drivers drove the night shift. Because he owned his cabs he was leasing them out to drivers and making money in the process.

    I was immediately taken by this idea and wondered why I did not know of this opportunity before. At that time I was a working single mom but mainly working from pay check to paycheck and the opportunity sounded like the kind of passive income idea I was looking for. So, I decided to invest in the opportunity and had won a white 2003 Ford Crown Victoria from govdeals.com, an online government auction site. After putting $700 worth of work to fix it, I had managed to lease my taxi to the local taxi cab company who was able to paint the taxi for me and put a driver in it. Within less than a month my taxi was earning me $250 extra dollars a week. Which brought in $1000 a month in passive income! The best part was that I didn't have to drive it myself.

After two months I made my money back for the repairs and purchase of the car that I bought at auction and the taxes I paid to get the title in my name. Also I didn't have to feel like I was living from pay check to pay check anymore and a driver got to earn money as well as the company that I leased the car to.

So how does this usually work? You supply the car as a lease to the taxi cab company. The taxi cab company pays the insurance on the car. Because they have to pay the insurance and they provide the dispatch service for the drivers they charge the drivers a weekly fee. The driver's earnings can vary but most report making in the hundreds per week because of the need for their taxi cab service and the efforts of dispatch. The drivers in turn pay you at the end of that week the flat rate that the company agrees to lease the car for at a rate of $200 to $250/week depending on the taxi cab company. This is a cash based business so proper record keeping and filing taxes is highly recommended to prevent you from getting audited. Remember the taxi cab company pays taxes too so Uncle Sam will know you're getting paid.

Some people even go as far as owning their own fleet of cars and start their own taxi cab business. That takes more work and has more liability but the opportunity does exist. If this is what you choose to do because maybe you have the startup capital to do it, check the local licensing laws in your state to see what is needed to start your fleet. Consider researching insurance and liability plans and choose a niche and uniform set of cars so you can stand out from the rest. For example, Black Cab or Green Cab for the green energy enthusiasts with a fleet of electric cars or Yellow Cab if you'd like to stay traditional. If you are like me however and you have no desire to drive a taxi, leasing your car can bring you a decent amount of passive income and an opportunity to have even more cars up and running on the road as taxis.

INDEPENDENT VERIFIER

When I first got started in background screening I was an employee at Sterling Testing Systems in New York City and that's where I learned a lot about the employment background screening industry. What I learned in this business as well was that there are many external verifiers that work from home who are paid to verify the information that job applicants put on their employment application. You'll be surprised how many people stretch the truth on job applications in order to get a job and don't realize that there are people behind the scenes who literally check up on them by calling and verifying their contacts.

Many businesses and staffing agencies use third party background screening companies to check employment backgrounds. Even other industries utilize background screeners for example landlords and property managers check rental and credit histories.

So after soaking up as much knowledge about the industry, I started Allied Background Screening Solutions, a small online based business that I started in my bedroom. My investment was $1000 for a software that allowed employers and staffing agencies to privately go online through my own website and submit orders for criminal background checks for a flat fee of $49.95 which would go through an automated system and provide a report on the person of interest within a two to three day turn-around time.

TEN UNIQUE SIDE HUSTLE IDEAS FOR THE NEW YEAR

Turn-around time is the amount of time it takes for a criminal report to get back to the client requesting the report. In this business turn-around time is important. This business doesn't require much time or energy and most software allow for privacy so that information like social security numbers and birth dates do not fall in the hands of the wrong people.

To make more money in this business you can also add other verification services that are not based online such as employment verifications and rental verifications to name a couple.

If you're going to get into this business I recommend getting it established as a limited liability company and setting up a separate bank account for business tax purposes. This is by no means a fly by night operation and should be treated as a business since sensitive information is involved. What I liked as well about this online business opportunity is that when I was ready to move on to something else, I was able to sell the business website for a profit instantly flipping the business opportunity without loss and risk.

There are a few things worth mentioning that you need to know with this business. This is important because it can either make or break your entire operation. First I recommend getting the proper business license to operate even if you decide to run this operation from home. I've already mentioned forming an LLC and the business bank account. The one thing I did want to mention is that if you or someone in your household has a criminal record you may not want to start a business as an independent verifier because of the aforementioned sensitivity of information that will be coming in from your clients about prospective job or rental applicants.

While most of the information that is transmitted between you and your clients are usually secured, sometimes social security numbers are not fully masked on applications. This should not be in the hands of anyone who has been convicted of criminal activity involving theft, financial fraud and anything deemed a liability or issue of mistrust within your operation.

Hopefully this doesn't shy you away from starting this type of business it can be very profitable and has major potential for turning into a full time big business venture.

ANTIQUE MALL DEALER

When you think about selling antiques, what usually comes to mind is selling on Ebay and selling at flea markets but you can be an antique dealer and not have to sell anything at all. As a matter of fact you can pay someone else to manage, display and sell your antiques for you at a local antique mall. All you have to do is lease one of their spaces and they do the rest. Have you ever been to an antique mall or market? These typically look like a very large retail space with individual sections of different antique collections owned by different antique collectors that set up shop in the antique mall. The person who runs the mall runs the register and takes the sale of the item on behalf of the antique dealer in their absence. This is another popular passive income opportunity and with shows like Antique Road Show paving the way, it's becoming even more profitable of a business for small antique collectors.

Normally when I go antiquing I get a lot of good finds at Goodwill, Salvation Army, yard sales, estate sales, the community thrift and online. ShopGoodwill.com is a great place to reach other goodwill stores that are far away from you as well. Some collectors focus on glass, others on tin and some even like porcelains or art. Antiquing can be a lot of fun and sometimes you even find items that you yourself won't try to part with. For example I've become quite attached to German Steins, tea sets, Japanese Satsuma porcelains and stained glass. I've even managed to obtain a brass plate of John F. Kennedy's image which I purchased in excellent condition for five dollars and a 1921 Remington Standard typewriter that I bought for under fifty dollars which I have in my personal collection.

It is recommended that you do some research on antiquing so you would be better at it. Kovel's Antique Collectibles and Price Guide is a helpful resource along with Antique Trader. There's no course that exists that I know of that can help you in this field but there's no better learning opportunity than through experience. Take a trip to one of those antique markets and don't be afraid to talk to the people there and ask them what's hot and what's not. Inquire with the managers about what the spaces cost and look around to see what your competitors are selling.

I also recommend a niche. I cannot tell you how many times I've visited a collector's booth only to be overwhelmed with a whole lot of nothing or bins of what appears to be garbage. In this business the old adage "a niche will make you rich" greatly applies. It's best that if you like glass then specialize in collecting and selling glass. Fenton and Carnival Glass are popular and profitable choices. If you like dolls then consider a niche in dolls, doll houses and the like. Maybe you like porcelains. With porcelains, the niche possibilities are endless from miniature tea sets to decorative plates, vases and cookie jars.

There's a collector out there for just about anything and a market to get your antiques sold. So you can make it a hobby or make it a business either way, make antiquing a fun way to earn extra cash.

SOCIAL NETWORK PUBLISHER

Today we live in a very computer mediated society and social media has taken over the scenes with everyone showcasing either their talent or hobbies to a large number of people. We never imagined just how much the internet and advertising would change when we were first introduced to the world-wide web. With sites like Twitter, Youtube and Facebook there's a number of people making money online more than ever before and all they have to do is advertise a product on their channel and get paid based on the number of subscriptions, views or likes. The more popular you are on youtube for example, the larger your subscriptions the more money you can earn in advertising products. Plus there's the extra added bonus of receiving free promotional products as well.

One of these most notable sites that offer this opportunity is MyLikes.com! According to mylikes.com, they are the largest content and social advertising platform in the world that use regular people to advertise products for their clients by driving millions of clicks to their website. Who ever created MyLikes was a genius and they created an opportunity for people on youtube and twitter and other platforms to make extra cash!

All you have to do is go to mylikes.com and sign up as a Publisher to start earning money by promoting products you like. There's an art to this, don't start bombarding your subscribers with buy this and buy that requests, instead, do a product review and be honest. Your subscribers will appreciate you for keeping it real and will trust future reviews that you make on products you are promoting.

Other opportunities exist in affiliate marketing programs with companies such as LinkShare and Commission Junction. Both of these companies allow you to sign up as a Publisher whereby you can apply as an affiliate promoting business products and services for a commission.

In addition to social networks, you can also promote products and services through a personal website. Many of these affiliate programs if not all of them, provide links that you can add to your website which can attract clicks from prospective buyers of these services.

If there's one piece of advice that I can give and a major what not to do when it comes to this type of side hustle it's don't sell yourself out. If you don't believe in a particular product or service then don't sell it. You can't be a good product or service promoter if you don't believe in the product or service you're selling.

BROKER PRICED OPINIONS
(For Agents and Non-Agents)

Broker Priced Opinion or BPO is a money making opportunity commonly found in the real estate and asset management industry. A BPO is an asset management tool used by mortgage companies and lenders whereby an estimated value of property is obtained.

Many real estate agents can get started in BPO's by simply applying as a BPO agent with Fannie Mae and Freddie Mac for example or other private valuation companies such as Protek and CoreLogic and Keystone Asset Management to name a few. Many agents use automated BPO systems to mass produce valuations which does all the comparable property searches and data input for them. The more BPOs you do of course the more money you can make.

BPO's can pay anywhere from $50.00 for an exterior BPO to $75.00 per interior BPO or more depending on the home valuation. Many of the homes are either bank owned or what is known as REO's, currently on the market as a short sale or unfortunately soon to be foreclosed on.

So how does BPO's really work? Let's say you signed up with ProTek. ProTek sends out a property for valuation at 100 Main street and wants you to do a drive by BPO. They'll pay you $50.00 when it's complete. All you have to do is. Go to 100 Main Street.

Take a picture of the front of the property and if it's vacant you can also take pictures of the back exterior, a picture of the street to the left, a picture of the street to the right and a picture directly across from the house to give them an idea of the neighboring homes on the block. This process takes less than five minutes if it's an exterior BPO. Then once you're back on your computer, you'll upload the pics and provide information on comparable current listings, recent properties that sold in the area and how much you believe based on that information the property you valuated is worth in that current market.

What if you're not a real estate agent? Can you make money in BPO's? But Of Course! Many real estate agents are far too busy showing houses to do drive by BPO's and it isn't illegal for you to take pictures on their behalf so consider marketing yourself to local real estate agents as a BPO Photographer. This unique idea makes for a great side hustle. There's a vast amount of information on how to take these pictures and from what angles. But once you practice taking a few valuation pics of your own home, you can advertise yourself as a BPO assistant taking photographs at locations for the BPO Agent. Now how's that for getting a piece of that real estate pie?

You want to know the best part? No technical skills are needed. You don't have to edit pictures, A simple digital camera will do just fine and all you really need is a reliable vehicle to drive to locations and a few of your agent's business cards at the ready in the event a homeowner asks questions as some of them do.

Here's the bonus and I can tell you this as a former real estate and BPO Agent... you can also offer your services as a real estate sales photographer and start taking additional assignments of photographing properties that your agent is listing for sale. To those agents who would like to get into BPOs, I've included a list of BPO Companies toward the end of this book to get you started.

LIST OF BROKER PRICED OPINION COMPANIES

Here you can research the following companies to sign up as a Vendor, Partner or BPO agent. Different companies use different terms for their representatives. This list was created the last time I was a BPO agent myself so please note that links do change from time to time and some businesses may have closed.

Advanced Collateral (aka Valuation Support Services) https://www.vss20.com
Advent REO http://www.adventreo.com
America's Infomart Inc. http://www.quickbpo.com
American Home Mortgage Svcs https://ahmsi3.com
Appraisal Bank http://www.appraisalbank.org
ASD America http://www.asdamerica.com
ASGBPO http://www.asgbpo.com
Asset Disposition Management http://www.admreo.com
Asset Valuation and Marketing http://www.assetval.com
Atlantic Pacific REO http://www.atpacreo.com
Atlas REO Services http://www.atlasreo.com
Bankers Asset Mgmt. http://www.bamreo.com
BPO Direct (Freddie Mac) http://www.bpodirect.com
BPOs Online http://www.bposonline.com
Brighton Real Estate Services http://www.brightonreo.com

TEN UNIQUE SIDE HUSTLE IDEAS FOR THE NEW YEAR

Broker Price Opinion http://www.brokerpriceopinion.com
California REO Mgmt. http://www.calreo.com
Carrington Mortgage Services http://www.carringtonms.com
CBC Innovis http://www.cbcinnovis.com
Central State Appraisers http://centralstateappraisal.com
Clear Capital http://www.clearcapital.com
Coldwell Banker/NRT REO Experts http://www.reoexperts.net
CoreLogic http://www.farvv.com
Corporate Asset Management http://www.camreo.com
Corporate Valuation Services Inc. http://www.provalu.com
Crest REO http://www.crestreo.com
Dinwiddle Property Services http://www.dinproserv.com
DISPOSolutions https://www.disposolutions.com
eAppraiseIT http://www.eappraiseit.com
Elam REO Services http://www.elamreo.com
eMortgage Logic https://www.emortgagelogic.com
ETCREO Management http://www.etcreo.com
Evaluate USA http://www.evaluateusa.com
eValuation Solutions https://www.evalonline.com
Financial Asset Services http://www.fasinc.com
First American REO http://www.firstamreo.com
FISERV http://www.fiservlendingsolutions.com
Go BPO http://www.gobpo.com
Goodman Dean http://www.goodmandean.com
Green River Capital http://www.greenrivercap.com
Hansen Quality http://www.hanqual.com
iMortgage Services http://www.imortgageservices.com
Inside Valuation http://www.insidevaluation.com
Instant BPO http://www.instantbpo.com
JVI REO http://www.jvireo.com
Keystone Asset Management
https://www.keystonebest.com/mvc/home
LAMCO http://www.lendersreo.com
LPS Lenders Services Inc. http://www.lenderservice.com
Mainstreet Valuations https://www.mainstreetval.com
National foreclosures http://www.nationalforeclosures.com
National Listing Agent Mngt. http://www.nlamreo.com
National REO http://www.nreo.com
National Vendor Mngt Svcs http://nvms.com
Nationwide BPOs http://www.nationwidebpos.com

Premier Real Estate Services http://www.premierbpo.com
Pro Tek Services http://www.protk.com
Rels Valuation http://www.relsvaluation.com
REM Corporation http://www.remusa.com
REO America http://www.reoam.com
REO Connection http://reoconnection.com
REO Illinois http://www.reoillinois.com
REO Nationwide http://www.reonationwide.com
REO Network http://www.reonetwork.com
REO.com http://www.reo.com
Safe Harbor Collateral Solutions http://www.safeharborus.com
Secure Collateral http://www.equitynational.com
Secured Lending Services http://www.securedlendingservices.com
Single Source Property Solutions http://www.singlesourceproperty.com
Sky Hill REO http://www.skyhillreo.com
Snow Enterprises LLC http://www.webinspections.com
SunTrust Mortgage http://www.suntrustmortgage.com
Transcontinental Valuations http://www.transconvalue.com
TREOnet http://www.treonet.com
US Real Estate Services http://www.usres.com
USA Valuation Services http://www.usavaluationservices.com
ValuAmerica http://www.valuamerica.com
Valuation Partners http://www.valuationpartners.com

TIME TO GO GET YOUR SIDE HUSTLE STARTED

So now you have in your hand ten awesome ideas for a side hustle small business. There are so many more that exist that you can imagine you just have to think of a need to fill and fill it. Fear is the only thing that can hold you back from fulfilling your goals of starting your dreams.

If there is one thing that I'd like for you to take away it's that you don't have to allow your life to blow in the direction that the wind blows. That is, because the economy may determine what your employer wants to pay you, that doesn't mean that you can't take total control over your earnings. Ultimately we all have the tools in front of us to get moving with our own personal ventures we just have to take the time to get it started.

If you feel as though you lack business know how, there's tons of free open courseware online from places such as Udemy.com or MIT Open Courseware that offer free courses. Youtube as mentioned before is an excellent learning resource and none of these platforms cost a thing. You take advantage of these resources if you want to increase your skills in the area of business if you don't have the know-how.

Because you've taken this step in reading this book, that tells me that you are ready to take charge of your financial future and you're ready to make a change in your life. So what are you waiting for? Let's get started!

ABOUT THE AUTHOR

Dana Sage has started multiple businesses in fields ranging from Real Estate to Daycare Operations, Makeup Artistry, Antiquing and Background Screening to name a few. She has an educational background in Finance and Human Development.

www.ingramcontent.com/pod-product-compliance
Lightning Source LLC
Chambersburg PA
CBHW070725180526
45167CB00004B/1619